# The Story of
# THE HULA

**Rob Waring,** *Series Editor*

HEINLE
CENGAGE Learning™

Australia • Brazil • Japan • Korea • Mexico • Singapore • Spain • United Kingdom • United States

# Words to Know

This story is set in the United States (U.S.), in the state of Hawaii [həwɑi]. In the story, you will read about the city of Hilo [hilou].

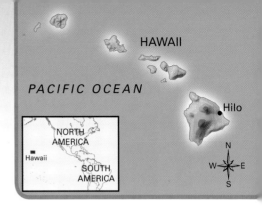

HAWAII

PACIFIC OCEAN

Hilo

NORTH AMERICA

Hawaii

SOUTH AMERICA

N W E S

**A** **The Hawaiian Islands.** Read the paragraph. Then, match each word with the correct definition.

Hawaii is a group of islands in the Pacific Ocean. The islands are in a tropical area, which means that it is very hot there. Hawaii has the sea all around it, so it has many beautiful beaches. It is also a land with an ancient history and culture. Long ago, Hawaii had kings and queens that ruled the island. They were very powerful leaders. There are many legends in Hawaii as well. They tell interesting stories about the past.

**1.** island _____       **a.** a woman ruler

**2.** sea _____       **b.** very old

**3.** tropical _____       **c.** a large body of water

**4.** beach _____       **d.** an old story from the past

**5.** ancient _____       **e.** an area of sand or stones next to the sea

**6.** queen _____       **f.** from or in the hottest parts of the world

**7.** legend _____       **g.** an area of land that has water all around it

## B  Hula Dancers. Read the sentences. Then complete the paragraph with the underlined words.

The hula (hulə) is a type of <u>dance</u>.
A *halau* (həl<u>au</u>) is a school where they teach the hula.
Hula dancers wear special <u>costumes</u>.
Hawaiian people dance the hula at special events called <u>festivals</u>.
<u>Spiritual</u> means with strong feelings or beliefs.

In Hawaii, the hula is a very important traditional (1) _____.
It's more than three hundred years old. Nowadays, Hawaiians
dance the hula at (2) _____. For some, the hula is a
(3) _____ dance that they relate to personal beliefs and
feelings. People can learn the hula at a (4) _____. Most hula
dancers wear beautiful (5) _____ and put flowers in their hair.

A Tropical Island

Hawaiian Hula Dancers

Hawaii is a truly beautiful place. Most people know Hawaii for its lovely beaches and its warm sea. However, Hawaii is also a land full of legends. Several old stories have existed for many years on these tropical islands. One of the oldest legends is about a special dance called the hula, which started here more than three hundred years ago.

One hula teacher tells the story of how the dance started. "The hula started, as far as legend tells it, when **Hi'iaki**[1] and her good friend **Hopoe**[2] went down to the beach. And then, when they were there, they noticed the waves…and they **imitated**[3] the waves. And then they started to use their hands… like **portraying**[4] the waves. That's how the hula started."

---

[1]**Hi'iaki:** [hɪʔiɑki]
[2]**Hopoe:** [hoʊpoʊaɪ]
[3]**imitate:** behave in a similar way as someone or something else
[4]**portray:** show; act like

sea

waves

beach

## Sequence the Events

**What is the correct order of the events?**
**Read page 9, then number 1 to 4.**

_____ The queen banned the hula.

_____ The religious people were surprised.

_____ Dancers performed the hula
in secret.

_____ Religious people came to Hawaii.

However, not everyone has always liked the hula. In 1820, very **religious**[5] people from Western countries came to Hawaii. They were surprised by the hula because the dancers were not wearing many clothes. The visitors were so surprised, that they asked the queen of Hawaii to **ban**[6] the dance.

After that, Hawaiians were not allowed to perform the hula in public for almost sixty years. But that did not mean the dancing stopped. Many dancers still performed the hula **in secret**.[7] The dance was always there.

---

[5]**religious:** believing in God or gods
[6]**ban:** not allow; stop
[7]**in secret:** not seen or known about by most people

Years later, things have changed. At the moment, there is a renewed interest in Hawaiian culture throughout these islands. People of all ages want to study the ancient culture. They want to learn how to dance the hula.

This interest has resulted in an increase in the demand for hula lessons. So, more and more people are attending *halaus*. *Halaus* are special schools that teach the hula in the traditional way. These schools also teach the traditional values, and **discipline**, [8] that go along with the dance.

---

[8]**discipline:** rules and control

The hula isn't an easy dance to do. First, the dancers must work very hard to learn it. Then, they have to practise for many hours. If they want to perform the dance for other people, they must be ready and well prepared.

One person who can help dancers prepare is **Kumano Palani Kulala**.[9] Kumano is a hula teacher. For him, the dance is a way to bring the best of ancient Hawaiian culture to people today.

---

[9]**Kumano Palani Kulala:** [kumɑnoʊ pəlɑni kulɑlə]

Kumano says that the dance is not really about the body. He feels that it's more about the mind. He also believes that it's a very spiritual dance. He explains his feelings: "...the hula is more...not so much a **physical**[10] thing, but more of a **mental**[11] and a spiritual thing. For [new dancers], the dancing means very little, because for Hawaiians today, many of them don't speak the [Hawaiian] language. So, what I try to do is to bring to mind the reality that they see today."

[10] **physical:** of the body
[11] **mental:** of the mind

**Fact Check: True or false?**

1. Dancers have to practise a lot.

2. Kumano Palini Kulala is a hula teacher.

3. The hula is only a physical thing.

4. Many Hawaiians don't speak the Hawaiian language.

With the help of people like Kumano, the hula has become an important part of Hawaiian life and culture once again. Because of this, there are now many hula festivals in Hawaii. Every year, the most important hula **competition**[12] happens in the city of Hilo. Dancers from all of the Hawaiian Islands come together at this festival. The festival is held in the name of a legendary Hawaiian king. This king helped to return the ancient hula dance to its place at the centre of Hawaiian culture.

In the competition, of course the **judges**[13] look at the way the dancers dance. But they look at more than just that. They also look at the dancers' costumes and their style. The way the person wears a skirt, the colour of his or her costume, and the flowers they wear are all very important.

---

[12] **competition:** an event in which people try to be the best and win
[13] **judge:** someone who decides which person or thing wins

Today in Hawaii, the ancient hula dance is definitely not done in  secret; it's a part of everyday life. It's once again a tradition that people can practise and perform often. It's a tradition that they can see at various festivals. And hopefully, it's a tradition that will continue for years and years to come.

# After You Read

1. The hula was created _____ three hundred years ago.
   A. more
   B. exactly
   C. over
   D. less than

2. Which is a good heading for page 6?
   A. Two Girls Watch the Sea and Make a New Dance
   B. Teacher Creates Ancient Hula Story
   C. Legend of Hula Dance Began in the Sea
   D. Sea Imitated Hula

3. The religious visitors in 1820 probably came from:
   A. Hawaii
   B. Asia
   C. Europe and the U.S.
   D. Hilo

4. What did the hula dancers do after the queen banned the dance?
   A. They stopped dancing.
   B. They danced in secret.
   C. They started wearing more clothes.
   D. They performed for everyone.

5. On page 9, 'they' in paragraph one refers to:
   A. hula dancers
   B. the queen
   C. Hawaiians
   D. the visitors

6. The writer thinks that learning the hula is:
   A. easy work
   B. simple work
   C. difficult work
   D. surprising work

**7.** Kumano believes that the body is the most important part of hula.
   **A.** True
   **B.** False

**8.** What happens in Hilo every year?
   **A.** a big dance event
   **B.** a competition with judges
   **C.** a festival for a legendary king
   **D.** all of the above

**9.** On page 16, the word 'return' in paragraph one means:
   **A.** bring back
   **B.** continue
   **C.** go home
   **D.** organise

**10.** In the competition, the judges look for more than _____ a person dances.
   **A.** which
   **B.** how
   **C.** who
   **D.** when

**11.** What is the purpose of this story?
   **A.** to show tradition is important
   **B.** to celebrate a great Queen
   **C.** to teach people how to dance the hula
   **D.** to show that competitions are easy

# TRAVEL News
# CARNIVAL IN TRINIDAD

C arnival in Trinidad is one of the longest and happiest parties you could possibly attend. It starts in December and goes on until February. Every year people from all over the world come to this festival. They come to enjoy the great music and unusual food. If you decide to visit Trinidad, you may also have the chance to join the party on this beautiful tropical island.

Kings and Queens Costume Competition

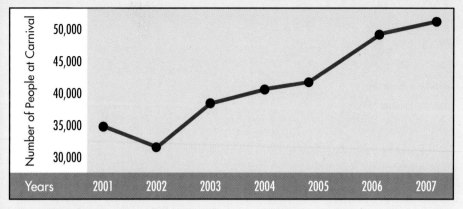

Rising Attendance at Carnival in Trinidad

The main events happen at the end of Carnival. One of the most interesting events is the 'Kings and Queens Costume Competition.' All of the musical groups from the Carnival have their own king and queen. This couple then appears in costume with their musical group. The costumes cost hundreds of U.S. dollars and take many months to create. Some of them are over thirty feet high! Every year, judges choose the best costumes.

In the beginning, Carnival had a religious purpose and the local churches organised the events. However, the people of Trinidad and Tobago originally came from many different cultures. Because of this, they soon began to incorporate other traditions. These traditions came from different parts of the world including South America, Africa, England, France, and India.

This makes Carnival one of the most colourful and varied festivals in the world. It also explains why people from so many different countries choose to attend Carnival.

The latest data shows that attendance at Carnival has risen almost every year since 2001. The figures show an increase from around 35,000 people in 2001 to over 50,000 in 2007. Six out of ten visitors to the country come from the United States, Canada, or the United Kingdom. Carnival attracts many people between December and February, but the island's beautiful beaches and sea bring thousands more visitors all year round.

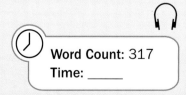

**Word Count:** 317
**Time:** _____

# Vocabulary List

**ancient** (2, 10, 13, 16, 18)

**ban** (8, 9)

**beach** (2, 4, 6)

**competition** (16)

**costume** (3, 16)

**dance** (3, 4, 6, 8, 9, 10, 13, 14, 15, 16, 18)

**discipline** (10)

**festival** (3, 16, 18)

*halau* (3, 10)

**imitate** (6)

**in secret** (8, 9, 18)

**island** (2, 4, 10, 16)

**judge** (16, 17)

**legend** (2, 4, 6, 16)

**mental** (14)

**physical** (14, 15)

**portray** (6)

**queen** (2, 8, 9)

**religious** (8, 9)

**sea** (2, 4)

**spiritual** (3, 14)

**tropical** (2, 4)